HOME AND AWAY

HOME AND

AWAY

Steve Ellis

BLOODAXE BOOKS

ISBN 1 85224 027 X

First published 1987 by
Bloodaxe Books Ltd,
P.O. Box 1SN,
Newcastle upon Tyne NE99 1SN.

Bloodaxe Books Ltd acknowledges
the financial assistance of Northern Arts.

Typesetting by Bryan Williamson, Manchester.

Printed in Great Britain by
Tyneside Free Press Workshop Ltd, Newcastle upon Tyne.

For Joanna and Edwin

Acknowledgements

Acknowledgements are due to the editors of the following publications in which some of these poems have appeared: *The Fiction Magazine, The Gregory Awards Anthology 1981 & 1982* (Carcanet–Society of Authors, 1982), *The Literary Review, New Poetry 4* (Hutchinson–Arts Council/P.E.N., 1978), *Oxford Poetry* and *Poetry Review*. 'Temporary Jobs' was broadcast on BBC 2, and 'At a Grandparent's Funeral' and 'Roles' on *Poetry Now* (BBC Radio 3).

Contents

Temporary Jobs

Uncle James was a suburban astronomer, mis-married
in his youth. Occasionally he got off,
from papering alcoves and fitting laminated
surfaces, to ponder on the presence
of night, up in an unused bedroom.
He affronted the sky with binoculars.
They said he was snooping in houses
for women undressing, shutting their curtains
on his ancient quest. Alone with the All,
the suburb righteously smoothed its skirts beneath him.

His mystic charts, how an old Arab name
would flare in his head like freedom!
'Al-gehiroth, delta-Lyrae', he crooned
at the map of yellow nail-heads on his knees.
High, high up, beyond the pouting street-lights,
Orion with a cosmos in his belt
fights back the charging Bull forever, Uncle James
looking on, entering in his notes
a Leonid shower across the moon,
that swam to earth in sparkling cinders.

He lay in bed thinking, next to his wife's back.
I am an antique Arab myself. Up there
a court of primal riddles
reclines along our rooftops, a repository
of ageless heroes overarching us. Up there
eternity is always in our faces. They would slip
from protests at the price of bread
to gabblings against him, but he didn't care;
a man who knows all this
fits surfaces differently to other men.

At a Grandparent's Funeral

Divergent endeavours met on her sideboard,
focussed to a family: a jumble of cousins
not seen by one another for a decade
were neighbours of the big clock and husband
dead forty years, pewter-framed.
Across the room, an armchair gobbled her up,
a sheath of angles sprouting a perm,
her glasses imprisoning the window's shot
of wandering sky through hours of old age
till she waded to welcome us . . .

I recall this, head lowered. The vicar
prays on for the blank space's soul
that he fills in with her name, Annie.
The curtains close over gleaming wood
to rows of crying; the cousins are reunited.
Afterwards we eat dry sandwiches
in her honour, each of us pleased
the different disclosed adulthoods confirm
he's getting on best. Once back at home
my father sits silent above the chaos
of games and children across the carpet,
as if he watches his own wife and sons
play with the kids inside a glass case
he drifts past into endless seas
now Love's finely-wrought anchor has snapped.

The Age of Innocence

At school, we all had to pick a plague
out of Exodus; round the table,
elbowing each other in innocent enthusiasm,
the girls drew mostly feverish first-borns, the boys
boils and frogs; while I fancied the river of blood.
Except some little s-d had pinched all the reds.
So I did locusts: houses, palm trees, pyramids
carefully laid in; arabs arranged unsuspecting,
a sudden camel; stood back, aimed, and

FURIOUS blitzings with the pencil,
God's green pepper milling down,
marvellously missing Moses,
tucked with his rifle in the margin.
Our work went up round the walls, whereon
the headmistress appeared
in a clap of lavender,
benign and gratified,
and scattered gold stars like benedictions.

Muncaster Cricket Club 1882

Three rows of hard suspicious eyes
beneath ringed caps, above moustaches;
an umpire in a prophet's beard and gown;
beside the boots the opening pair
in symmetrical languor along the grass.
Skating their names I notice a gap
and circle the face that goes with it,
looming because forgotten. This wink
of history is a title more immense
than the harmless double-barrels all around it.

And studying him, I see the reason:
the shaven walls of the head, cheek-bones
like struts inside the mouth, the eyes
black drills where all the other eyes
seem furry now, distracted – after it was shot
did he slink off at its sepia edges
to butcher the baby, or bully a path
through a forest of straps and underskirts,
smothering her afterwards, slipping away free
in the dark streets of the dark century?

Between sloping shoulders of team-mates
he stands in the dock after ninety years.
Mine is the first face he's looked into
since then. I leaf through the next decades
but am followed by his freedom, even when
I put the book back in its place.
It tilts one end of the bookshelf
like the pans of the archangel's balance.

Sour Grapes

Within these walks I inter my failure:
a good interview but not good enough.
A walled garden: mind has found here
a symbol of solace for centuries,
whenever man's world or worlds fell apart –
purity, peace, and perspective.

Here I find a place among
a society of work and song;
the daisies waiting on the bees,
the music-boxes in the trees,
the dust with wings, the butterfly
scribbling himself across the sky;
the chequerwork of leaves in light
like silver lotion to the sight,
concentrating everywhere
and past and future, to a square.

Yet never as now were these walks so threatened,
nor mind that plans and explains them.
I leave the garden, false microcosm
of a raging, bullying world. O brother earth,
you and I have no certain future;
let others read today's front page
trusting mortgage, marriage, and middle-age.

Roles

When he became D.H. Lawrence
he walked along feeling his thighs seething
with maleness, and awoke to the beauty
of his small head. Sitting in pub corners,
his bowels felt the turgid lust of woman
flash across the smoky interims, while a mane of power
strutted up his back. He crossed to the toilet
like an electric charge. But the sap
dried up: Normality idly swamped back
and smiled paternally.

Then he became Orwell –
neck-and-neck with exhaustion
he read through *three* Sunday papers
till all-round curiosity made his eyes ache.
Taking a rational, logical interest in
everything,
he had his hair cut short,
sensibly, shaved his Lawrentian stubble
and bought a pipe,
eagerly sliced
through friends' conversation
thirsty for the central issue,
but weary had to creep back into his own self, eventually.

Joyce was a bit more tricky,
but a vague commitment
to being generally obnoxious
seemed a starting point, plus the development
of whatever flagrant oddity he could muster.
He brushed up his vulgarities,
exposing them joyously at a drink's notice.
Contemplating elopement, his hateful self
floundered with him back
to his ownness heaped on the bank.

He looked his ownness in the eye,
this brown panel staring through
successive layers of paint. He promised it
his fidelity. In the wardrobe of tomorrows
Wilde and Kerouac and Dylan T.
hung on pegs like unused suits
while he wooed himself in the mirror.

A brief romance before future romancing.

Cornwall

I walked the aisle, between the menagerie:
Tudor pew-ends of foxes, dogs and hares
trained on the altar, their shapes sleeked
with years of hands over the black oak.
Outside, rain; rain to drown the village,
while I sat like Noah in his dark hold
silent among beasts, feeling light weaken
through the grey, saintless glass. The lady
– those cruel scars a flaw in the stone
or mad husband?, the vicar had riddled –
kept a look-out for the Last Day
from her corbelled crow's-nest in the choir.
Weather-bound I waited, reading the text
spread on the eagle; and then they entered,
along the nave, men, women and children
shaking the soil from ancient clothes,
from caps, leggings, jerkins, gowns, smocks,
filing into pews, settling for the sermon,
their eyes upon me as I began the verse:
'He that believeth shall be saved'.
I preached this theme to the full church;
to the bullet-snouted hounds, to the hares
with ears like flails along their backs
couched dimly beside the pews, aware
of a low chuckling, that strengthened:
I looked up to see the human faces
melt into muzzles, noses join with chins,
foreheads sink behind spreading ears,
hair streaming, rooting over skin,
and the laughter loud above my voice –
laughter in rows of gloating, goatish eyes,
hooting fur throats in cotton collars,
yelps, and kids' squeals, and foxes' shrieks.
I ran, between the pews and out into air,
outran the rain that coursed the roads
to the cottage; Maggie and John were getting tea
as if nothing had happened, but I knew.

'The Angling Times'

I come across this paper in a packing-case:
uncrumpling it, hoping for nudes,
am surprised, when the creases yield up
men in vistas, not breasts, tattooed,
oily, pullovered, each one lugged
briefly into fame by luckless landed lengths
of scaly substance hoisted lenswards, with
grins of capture back beyond the arm.
Page after page of them, the fish
disgraced in death, huge with boredom, the men
quiet but wily; the printed rhythm
of grin, arm, fish, grin, arm, fish
composed and complete. Could the end's
bombs and ruins end them? – having already
evacuated history, there, grey, anonymous,
undeniable, the fish, the faces.

An Encounter

The lady selling *Awake!* at Putney station
embodies the well-wrought life: locked
with a commuter in deep confession
her hands chop and square the air –
she is killing and trussing objections.

She is also moving in my direction
and the train is late.

So I brace myself for the clash:
the arc-light brilliancy of belief
versus dim Putney agnosticism.
The platform becomes a vast plain
and me the champion of ditherers,
displaying a doubtful device;
to that first crashing challenge
– 'Is there any meaning in life?' –
I counter strongly: 'Well, um . . . '

But it's all over: some benign spirit
has swept me to safety inside the train
and we shoot down the sink into London.
I peruse *Awake!*, trophy of battle,
among sleepy commuters; I see
badly-drawn dawns unlike any other,
humanity dancing out of its bed
to the chimes of a cosmic alarm-clock
to cuddle tigers in Eden. I think
I think these are admirable notions,
but rather ridiculous too:
thus maintaining the flexibility
of the balanced point of view.

At the Dante Alighieri Society Annual Dinner

Giovanni's had been booked for the evening;
shawled and suited amongst candlelight
we saluted Italy in Italy twice-removed:
Pirandello, Ravenna, the delicious *gnocchini*
that Dr Forester and wife fainted over
at the farm they rented every summer –
talk bobbed in the wine. I drifted
on the cosy redundancy of conversation
and aimlessly asked what *baccalà* was.

Dried cod cooked in milk, it seems
and ancient Fridays stirred inside me –
how strange to find her recipe here,
an exotic theme for cultured people!
And the fish-in-milk of childhood
became an enigma; plain, despised,
an unavoidable nourishing fact,
it now assumed mysterious ancestry,
a prince in hiding in a council kitchen.
So by grandmother's work-chapped elbow
I saw her standing, a small girl
with flour and ribbons in her hair
inheriting the migratory meals of Europe
that arrive by untraceable routes.

1977

A late summer evening in Muswell Hill:
pale sun in a rosy sky, like life itself
in Muswell Hill – placid and abstract,
or only pursuing remote excesses
behind depths of well-trained windows.
Prematurely slippered, I play my part
in this mild pantomime: acting neighbour
in a land where there are no neighbours,
I'm chopping at the garden hedge.

And really it could be poetry itself,
July twilight preceding a young moon:
midges dancing Arcadia, faint scents
floating off the gardens, an enormous
tranquil suspense. It could be,
but isn't. Poetry means possibility –
as all Muswell Hill unassumingly assumes
the norm of non-eventfulness
I'm here, chopping at the garden hedge.

Cup of tea, radio, landlord's rusty shears.
Radio 3 has a quaint sense of humour,
spraying this scene with a dramatisation
of *Paradise Lost*. I lop the high stalks
over next door's path; 'Him who disobeys
Me disobeys' rolls out across the avenues.
Rosy late summer. But now if the red sun
should sink hissing into a molten bath
while I'm chopping at the garden hedge

and the entire western sky burst apart,
the cosmic charioteer in clouds of glory,
the thunder of sword-toting angels –
well, the inhabitants of Muswell Hill
(practised in not perceiving lunatics
all over London) would faintly twitch
their curtains a shade or two closer;
and I – I'd turn with a strange fidelity
and chop on at the garden hedge.

Royal Wedding

If destiny had dressed one in the part
of earl or duke, or flag-flapping gran;
of teenage romancer, disgusted red,
or cynic enjoying his desert song,
or Poverty staring at peeling walls,
it would have been a knowable role;
but these liberal lines of discomfort,
attracted-bored, engrossed-detached,
invited to attend through a camera's eye,
kept out by walls of pageantry –
I've tried mastering these all day.

Great events are a self-assessment:
while armada beacons flared the country
little forty-watt bulbs of discontent
glimmered in a thousand rooms,
the unchosen women, the men with no choice.
London was at least palliative –
self slept among crowds and fireworks;
but as morning collapsed into afternoon
self woke: Occasion had sent it home
leaving it to ponder its place at the party.

Now it's midnight, and the pubs stay open.
Men like me sit in lonely rooms
uncovering doubts and fidelities,
belonging helplessly to England,
to England's unjust, maddening beauty;
and we soothe our sense of exclusion
as we creep to our everyday beds
in picturing a peaceful royal ravishing
among inaccessible Elgarian hills.

In the City Art Gallery, York

'Fame is no plant that grows on mortal soil'

I circle Reynolds & co., entering in good heart
their game of being impressive: pink grocers
and merchants locked proudly in cartouches;
a lawyer looking sternly from a letter,
distracted by the moth's-beat of the brush
from something more important. And one
in the real Grand Style, though on the cheap:
six hurried yards of wig, sword and tartans
parading before a splash of estate

storm and shadow; we stare each other out –
he has immobility, but I have volume.
Winning easily, I turn to go
leaving him unconcerned, even though
he no longer swells from a wall of velveteen
to thunder down a vista, having a corner
from the Corporation: workmen come each year
and shove him like a length of fence
to a fresh wall, uncovering at his back

a massive print of grime. As I leave,
the place is filling up. A mother rolls a pram
at random objects, seeing out the afternoon.
She passes a Flemish ham and oranges,
thinks about her husband's tea. A couple
of schoolkids romance by a radiator,
heads low, oblivious of a towering oil.
A family with the in-laws down
ooh and ah gamely at names and dates.

These'll be safe from painters. Their forms
won't outlast their voices and smells.
They will go ordinarily, as they came,
no browbeating their replacements, no clamouring
on a wall in the pickling-jar of art.

An early Baptist points the way out,
crude and beautiful after all the faces
falsified by fluent hands; long since exiled
with an axe from his lamb
and all the company of Heaven.

Man of Sorrows

If ever I meditate Incarnation
I shan't think of the huge thorns
The jumble of horses around the cross
Or a strip of fluttering loincloth;
No, I shall think of Trevor.

I met him one Easter afternoon
And had his story as the branch-line
Led us through scrapyard Yorkshire,
Ingrow, Keighley, Shipley, Leeds.
Compendium of Nature's off-days:
Weak eyes, beak nose, oily hair
Matted in directionless threads,
A miserly grant of jaw and neck
And forty, living with his dog
And an ageing Mother and Dad.
When he left to catch a Shipley bus
To some even more desolate destination
And two extra days of eventless holiday,
He turned to wave at me three times
As if such chances composed friendship;
Then set out belted into anorak
As the wind raged at his ankles
Flogging thin cloth around bone.

I rode on in horror at the sacrifice
Of being him: imagine some decree
To exchange one's friends and future
For that stifling, sterile circle!
So I shouldn't think of those things
Irrevocably beautified by art –
No, I should think of a man
Held at arm's length by all beauty.

On Re-Reading the Liverpool Poets

A grey sponge of drizzle swabs the Mersey;
a soft young soul roams along the bank
or watches from a bus, composing
unwithstandable *Invitations aux voyages*
to developing city schoolgirls:
    'My poetry-boat waits on the wave
    weighed with hampers of fish and chips;
    don't forget the vinegar, Marianne.'

God, the excitement of it at seventeen!
The future seemed a chain of bra's
deliciously yielding their contents,
culminating in that dark-haired One;
whom I was always planning to meet
in all-night parties' misty dawns
by meadow-flanked streams; she rises,
a Biba nymph, and our conjunction
is the climax of peace and truth.

I remembered this apparition last night,
reading of others dreaming it:
men for whom a wet bus window
might frame any masterpiece
in townscapes transfigured by love;
love never quite tempted to embark,
though softly nasal songs of jam butties
promised new earth,
Jam itself between the sliced decades.

The Rugby League Reporter Orders His Tomb in Halifax Cemetery

No son, don't go to any trouble –
that damp patch by your mother'll do
we used to keep tidy every Sunday
except when I had a match to cover:
green gravel chips, a bloom or two,
it's enough. A pilgrimage of pit towns
this life's been, the Wakefields, the Wigans,
Warringtons, these were my women:
beautiful names the tongue curls into
remembering decades of drizzly winters,
rusty stand-roofs slanted like caps
over lean crowds, views through goals
of terrace after terrace crawling off
with hearths as hot as laundries.
Thirty-five years of it son! The matches,
the pubs like people's front rooms,
only players and pensioners, crisp-packets,
ply counters, lino-scabs, the pink papers
with my reports . . . . Then the teams, son!
And the nights out we've had! By Hell,
we were down at Hull one Easter and –
well, never mind. I said, never mind.
This yearly getting round the Pennines
has more than been fair to me; a man's
to have a good few winters up his shirt
before he works out to very much.
I never thought there'd never be
a next season though; and now, thirty-five
gone! All them goals and grounds,
all them drinks, all . . . . all gone!,
son.

Heck, there'll be some games in Heaven!
The cherubim in gold and scarlet hoops,
seraphim in blue with silver trimmings,
letting you score your favourite try
over and over again: – Wigan, 1949:
Williams (the Newport panther) holding off

six defenders and a mad spectator.
I'll never forget it. That'll be mine!
. . . . If I were you, I'd just have me paved over,
don't fuss about grass or flower-beds;
you'll only keep having to weed it all
and your life's your own to get on with.
No, just lay me under that slope
looking at Leeds, within kickable distance
of what thirty-five years have meant:
the canals and chapels, smoke weaving up
out of all that brick, the roars
all about me at tackles and touch-downs
I'll be keeping an eye on – up above.

Our History Master

Our history master confronted the class
behind the triumphant gleam of his glasses
and advised us to dismiss Vietnam.
'Don't worry, boys,' he'd say. 'Central Europe,
that's always the axis. History informs us
World War III could only start from there.'
Then, safe with the key to Armageddon
he'd produce the bulky ageing folder
and dictate ninety minutes of Italian unity
or Bismarck, telling us when to put commas,
when to underline in red or green pencil,
generously duplicating his own crystal ball.

Our history master's in hale retirement now.
I can see him in his redecorated kitchen
at a breakfast of several marmalades
while his wife looks worried but faithful
as the first bombs explode in the distance.
No card-house of mattresses for him!
Aye, holding firm to his favourite flashpoint
he scans the paper, announcing
(as the ceiling flakes into his coffee)
'Don't worry, Mavis. Central Europe,' etc.

Elegy on the Fishing Correspondent

We couldn't believe it at first.
But when next week he still wasn't there
In homely limp trilby, his dot-paved face
Proudly encolumned at the page's head;
That the wits of the Deep
                    had faced his final challenge
Was gloomily comprehended.

Deprived of his guile at canals,
His seasoned assessment of streams,
We would doubtless err; lopped of these,
Life fights on. But the certainties
That vanished with him!
Front-page wars had come, had gone,
Crises, summits, governments, councils, deaths;
With watery wisdom once a week
He sat out such trivia unperturbed
As Permanence itself. Now his death
Bursts among his ostrich readers
Who search the paper desperately for sand.

To Ted Hughes

While I was cooking dinner
(some friends were coming round)
I thought I'd try your new cassette.

But you know how it is –
pans and peeling to synchronise,
recipes, and then the phone ringing:

you faded into far-off noise,
a low drumming
seeping from the lounge.

So going in there was a shock –
like opening the door of an oven
on your simmering concerns,

the rolling prophetic growl
that preached its elementals
to our carpets and chairs

unheard, unattended. To resume
butchering the chicken
seemed an act of homage;

but to eat it afterwards
with cutlery, wine and conversation
an act of sneaking treachery.

We should have daubed each other
all over with it
and danced among the bones.

York Minster

Silver early-morning silhouette,
   rectangular ghost
evaporating on the horizon
   as I walked to school.

Those were the sixth-form days,
   the thrill of the start
of the mind's future: books, plays,
   theories of love and sex,

the birth of articulation; and you
   shining like an emblem,
a hazy great emblem, of life
   waiting me across the fields

with all its promises. For to walk
   down your aisles under hedges
of flowering glass; to inspect
   pompous Latin tombs, grey slabs
of chill Norman floor, or review
   the screen's line of Gothic kings

was part of a gigantic romance,
   the threshold of a plot
starring me, university and women.
   You were all that York was not:

outside, bikes and coats, muffled greys
   of city life; here, no arcade,
no vista of columns, that she
   hadn't just left, trailing elusively
a trace of brown hair; no footstep
   behind, where I didn't turn
to see the sudden absence of her shape.

II

All the same, you Gothic bitch,
   you were always aloof,
impassive; thousands like me
   have come with conspiracies
and your clean stone soars enormous,
   washed of us all.

Or you teamed against me:
   middle-class club,
owned and staffed by middle classes,
   like the women I wanted
you were clear and cool, well-bred,
   stocked with silver;

your spaces rang with trained voices,
   choir of boy sopranos,
Oxbridge priests: my dreams focussed
   into having the dean's daughter
on the soft, green close
   while the organ pounded midnight mass.

III

Oh, I knew that 'heart of Yorkshire' stuff:
   coach-loads of Leeds grannies,
outings from west-riding mills, claiming
   their place inside a people's church;
and sometimes like a people's lad
   I've arsed about under your eaves.

Nights of disco's and drinking in York:
   girls, fish and chips
and kisses tasting of vinegar
   on a bench by the west front:

to look at arc-lit limestone
   and saints nodding down from ogees
makes a pretty interval
   in bouts of furious smooching;

when unknown perfumed armpits
   and breasts damp from dancing
and Decorated architecture
   mix into moments of glory.

You took me, like a neutral mother,
   in all my adolescent shapes,
whether I fingered female crevices
   or, studious, your own carving,
always the same, always radiant;
   and if I'd sunk completely
your smile wouldn't have changed,
   your shining supervision of York.

IV

Then these notes changed to sober –
    the gradual decline
of growing up. The plot thinned.
    I B.A.'d in art history
and cycled over Normandy
    visiting your sisters.

I learned a new language
    to appraise them in:
tierceron, clerestory, corbel –
    the practised wooer.

But it wouldn't work with you.
    Too near, too resented,
too full of earlier selves –
    I took my technique elsewhere.

Visiting York in vacations
    I felt like my own ghost,
stumbling between past and future,
    not seeing our separation
begin: you just leaked away
    during a decade of hard work.

Being eighteen leaked away too.
    Belief and emotion contracted,
wariness and snobbery grew.
    So we swapped lives:
I could look at your lovely body
    and feel unmoved as stone.

V

Now past thirty I approach you again,
  trying a new language,
trying to make up; settling for
  a placid, easily worn
relationship, a no-hard-feelings
  how've-you-kept truce;

congratulating you on another year
  in your permanence,
with wishes for the next five hundred;
  and since you ask,
while our paths were parting
  I've done quite well:

I love my wife, though not as I'd expected;
  I like my job
though it isn't what I thought;
  and existence –
well, it's not the Gothic garden
  I once knew,

being young, in the 60s, in York.
  You should learn that too:
I read last month of the party,
  your great roof down,
butt-ends of beams all over the floor
  smoked by the storm.

The time's gone for glory blazes,
  so follow after me:
I used to love storms, run mad
  in rain, not know
protest from praise; now I've learned
  to act my age.

Virgil
(after Pound)

MESSINA, 21 B.C.

Come on, damn it! Three long days
of provincial pentameters, prologuing me,
the climax, at the end. As with a cook
to friends, Imperator farms me out
round far-flung festivals, strengthening local talent
like a verse-stud. Day three:
hot southern hours we've had of Cn. Piso's
(talents thoroughly suited to invoicing grain)
Apollo-assisted (sic) 'Seven outside Thebes',
me waiting to read II, III, and
VI (by public request) . . . .

Finished at last! Sporting applause . . . .

Quiet, suddenly. My introduction. Usual honours,
and ('nectar-nursed') excesses.
Lapping it up,
the tanned amateur faces beneath me like a sea,
heartily awaiting this weary old
metropolitan to heave into his opus,
his standard, household opus . . . .

Ready, I think. Ready? Ready.

INFANDUM, REGINA, IUBES RENOVARE DOLOREM,
TROIANUS UT OPES ET LAMENTABILE REGNUM
ERUERINT DANAI, QUAEQUE IPSE . . . .

Cheers exploding.
God damn Imperator.

Found on a Junk Stall

A thirties schoolbook of *Standard French Poets*,
card-covered, ink-creased. In the front
the motto-crowned ladder of signatures
shows the notes on the poems are Dorothy's,
a few soft scrawls in the margins
in the same loose hand as her name:
ancient wisdom she'd taken down
to knit into essays and hand back in.

I can see the classroom as she writes:
the dense weight of a pre-war summer
drenching the rows of bent heads,
a teacher talking and a pen scratching
what I read now: 'Death's inescapability',
'the illusion of hope'; and with hopes
of sloughing gymslips for evening-gowns,
'a poem that shows the inadequacy of Love'.

I hope she lived to find these themes
good to get marks with but useless for life;
that she enjoys life still: the old dear
living next door seems happy enough
and might be her. Her son's down now:
his car in the drive, the rose-bushes
scrupulously circled with plots of lawn,
it all looks fine: just as if a child
had carefully built the street from a kit
(yet mightn't be trusted not to get bored).

Gentlemen Lift the Seat

I imagine such a notice
in heavy, black-painted brass
screwed into place on a steaming train,
superfluous to its trilbied and buttonholed
beholder; for whom blotting the woodwork
with ladies shuffling politely at the door
perhaps, would be an unthinkable acme
of horror.
I myself saw a man raise his hat
to a passing hearse, with a slight click of heels,
a barely perceptible bow,
while bundles of women
                lugged yokeloads of shopping
past and around him, grave on the pavement.
A decade's outmoded grace,
the bowing, hat-lifting, seat-lifting path
through his prime pursued there.

Newport, Gwent

No one notices Newport. But last night,
coming back over the bridge, with the rain
a soft mesh, and all the town lights
stepping down to the curve in the river,
the view seemed like some huge word,
like destiny, or bliss. We were riding
in triumph across the top of the world,
drawn by the dear bedraggled wings
of Newport – battery Swan of Usk!

Visiting Home

He weeds while I watch. I remember
how I always had to help him as a boy
and how bored I was seeding out
the summer's lines of different leaves.
I liked some bits: the bonfires,
the chance of digging up a roman coin,
but hung around mostly, required yet unnecessary,
blasting birds with my fingers
while he jawed green wisdom over council railings
where disciplined oblongs mirrored our own:
crops at right angles to a path running
straight down the middle; gardens combed
then parted like haircuts. I always wished
he'd grow flowers like other kids' dads,
but now I'm glad of his thrift: vegetables
embody the agreement between man and mud.

Later, me just into Lawrence, him just past
his prime, he was black-haired and silent,
deep amongst the greens, escaping
mother's chatter and her awful friends,
absorbing soil's intimate solace . . . .

Change now. I'm the age he was,
he nears the pension. In the evening
I wander in the garden when he leaves it:
the circling concrete houses hold a well
of winter air, grey and empty across
the estate's various shares of earth, dug,
deserted. Cats have come like litter,
and young men minus old skills
growing weedaria or prairies, while we keep
on with the old rules, the straight lines,
the trusted packets of seed as wilderness
waits in the wings. Though this doesn't upset;
rather, the corruption of cuttings,
the sure start of old age. Already
some forsythia holds fire in a corner,
some pampas grass looks fay by the rhubarb −

one day I'll come back to this: him standing
by a lawn rosy with advanced health,
sun silvering specs and dentures, wearing skirts
of cheap vague tarty hardy annuals.

York, 1980

In the ingle of an old city square
a bearded beadsman plays his flute;
a piper holds another paved place
like a chessman; all summer long,
street-theatres, soloists and morrismen
play among the walls and churches,
the antique bookshops, Tudor eating-houses
and hinged Dickensian shop-signs; all new,
or all newly-painted for the tourists.

But the locals can't be kept out: buses
still wheel them in from the council reserves
with their old shopping-bags and warm coats
innocent of fashion; they absorb
a few minutes' Consorte or dumb-show
en route to Boots or the market;
then go back to the kids and TVs,
the night-shifts and concrete houses,
rows of lace curtains and lamp-posts.

How totally sad, this show at prodding
a pre-war people into a future
itself devoted to an impossible past.
Today I watched a tambourined student
ribbing a shilling from one of those women
who sit ring-eyed in coffee-lounges
pulling for life on an afternoon cig.
He laughed heartily in his embarrassment,
she smiled palely in hers.

St Tropez: Yorkshire Impressions

Resolutely holding hands, they were found
sitting in judgement on these carefree sands.
Breasts swayed by, abandoned to the ploys
of Mediterranean breezes, schooled
in hot Antiquity, while the sun
thawed his equanimity. After an hour,
exhausted and overpowered by its vast
irrelevance to Doncaster, he cowered
beneath his hat-brim, dashed by new dimensions.

Calmer, he looked out. Along the edge of sea
a womanly arc of body intersected the horizon,
suckling the view with thrilled exposure,
furiously familiarising itself as Sandra
in his wondering eyes. Dragging her back,
and covering her dainties with a headscarf,
he sat in horror on his spur of beach,
not yet knowing from the look in her eyes
if he'd lost her like Orpheus
to some unthinkable, unimaginable kingdom.

St Francis's 'Cantico di frate sole'
done into Hollywood gangsterese

Boss, you got it all –
admiration, pull, status, the works –
it's all yours.

It's yours for being top –
there ain't no guy not too green
to mention you.

Thanks, for you and your organisation,
specially this guy Sun
who's always around with some light;

there's class stamped all over him,
a real smart guy –
he could only be one of your boys Boss.

Thanks, Boss, for these dames Moon and Stars,
platinum blondes in the night
you made real sweet.

Thanks, Boss, for this guy Wind
and the Weather boys, Air, Cloud, Sky,
bringing your gang the goods.

Thanks, Boss, for this dame Water –
she's a cute kid
and don't try to come over too big.

Thanks, Boss, for this guy Fire
who keeps his eye open after dark,
don't squeal and can handle himself.

Thanks, Boss, for old Ma Earth –
she looks after us real good,
always flowers and stuff around the joint.

Thanks, Boss, for the guys who take the rap
when you tell 'em,
that get roughed up and see trouble;

the smart guys know to keep their mouths shut
'cause you'll see to it Boss
they're on the payroll.

Thanks, Boss, for this cold dame Death
no guy can escape.
Nuts to the guys that die playing dirty.

Smart guys die in your good books.
There ain't no second show-down.

O.K. you guys, get prayin' –
say thanks to the Boss
and don't get big ideas.

To Philip Larkin
died 2 December 1985

I

You disappeared during a mild spell,
when all that seemed to be happening
or to be about to be happening
were merely familiar outrages,
the Middle East, child-abuse,
and policemen ambushed in Ulster.
Oh, the nightmare was still approaching,
shambling along in its endless way;
but there was no marvellous insanity
for you to raise your voice against,
no gala stage for the poet's speech;
and anyway, you'd tucked yourself
into a crude, acquiescent conservatism;
and anyway, you'd lost your voice.

II

I'd wanted you to die for years,
nursing myself for the big elegy
that would root on your ashes.
But you hung on and on, poemless,
like a man leaving the fire
to stray deeper into the night;
and the poem died in me too.
But in those heady early days
in York, the beginner's ecstasy,
Hull was the global meridian
all poetry was measured from;
and now you're gone, a flat blank gap
empty as East Yorkshire, sits on the map;
a gap life recomposes round
like the mouth round an absent tooth;
a death absorbed into life.

III

Anyway, you were always dead:
I fully shared your insistence
that you hadn't much existence –
your living was in your art.
Picture that ludicrous pilgrimage
whose shrine was your office,
your spectacles its relics;
to haunt the library precincts
and gate-crash your lunch-hour,
to launch you off on a tacky sea
of fierce young gush – absurd.
But still I needed you there
like a black hole emitting poems,
a Larkin of the imagination
reverenced across space.

And now the shock
is not that you're not:
you sang annihilation
like rightful destiny.
The shock is my calm
now the time has come.

IV

As a kid I made a kind of vow,
that I would never, absolutely never
put an end to my stamp-collection.
The joy of postmarks and perforations,
of hinges, of Victoria's cameo head
on the brightly coloured colonies,
these might fade for others, not for me.
At fourteen I sold it all cheap
to save for a guitar.

Practised in the ease of apostasy
I heard your death today on TV.

An Old Plate's Farewell to the Table
(after Geoffrey of Vinsauf)

Once in the springtime of my glaze
I lustily upshouldered, Atlas-like,
whole earths of meat and mash;
young and old in the gravy shallows
carved my face with strange signs
as fleeting as generations; and nights
I remember of a golden eminence,
when company directors stripped me bare
then spanked me with their knives and forks.

But my brothers gradually died away:
one was exiled to feed the cat,
one cracked in the oven, two more
shattered in the terrible kitchen war
of '79. I survived, an oddment.
Now, despite baptism twice a day
I begin to feel the shame of age
and am passed over. My old face fades:
Table, I depart, farewell.

Ad Patrem

So you've finally got a mortgage:
thirty years in council breeze-blocks
locked behind you for the last time –
the chubby brick bungalow all ready
to yield itself to your shiny Yale.
Redundancy was your greatest work
moneywise; but wheel your bike
in the wake of the furniture van
and reflect that my patrimony's gone,
squandered on transplantation.
Other poets have dads done in by Fate,
not feathering cosy corners;
lined men who gob in a bucket,
'thee' and 'thou' at the fire,
fill a room with rugged destiny.
I could have inherited it all,
being Yorkshire and working-class;
but though you'll still bike off t' club
to herd dominoes through a dour fog
of smoke and beer, remaining years
of roses and bowling-greens
seem your choice and my remembrance.
You might even get a little car!
Oh Dad, watch how you go
in retirement's renovating lake;
at least leave unchanged the bicycle-clips
for old sake's sake.

Sonnets from Putney

i

Opening the door to low evening mist
a huge vague moon and smell of smoke:
October is happening again
and I hardly saw summer was going.
Life is more and more train, desk,
desk, train, the London opportunity;
when I walked over the common yesterday
I dully sensed it was a year
since we arrived, a whole year's marvel
of programmed pitching through infinity,
frost to sunlight, green toasted red,
rich ceremonies of oak and harvest
lost as some promised land. Our year:
a grid of ringed rent-days.

ii

And yesterday the summer cricketers
were absurd thin ghosts, flitting over mud
and damp leaves red as jewels
or sinking up to imaginary ankles:
yet an image of fancied old age.
For since I'm shovelling all my days
into the grave of work, death could come
and rip me off as casually
as I rip dates from the calendar –
and then what hope of rich decay,
that rotting ratatouille of recall,
as scenes and faces of a lifetime
spill back on the floor of the mind
in delirious ferments of farewell?

The Late-Medieval Room, Sunday Morning

As another big-bellied bus rolls up
and spawns outside the Uffizi, inside
an earlier group more or less regard
the mighty Giotto, or their Italian guide
scraping her thoughts together in English.

There are several sad men, brought to share
the Renaissance of a spouse's later years,
anchoring wandering eyes with patient feet;
eyes that look on paintings, walls and people
without showing preference, that meet

similar eyes without recognition; and women
aglow with attention, or glowering with mistrust
at their guide's hair and handbag, who drifts
anecdotally on: 'Now Giotto warz a shepherd-boy,
one day he warz drorring a sheeeep . . .'

and they've gone. The Virgin remains,
massive, unchanged, her delighted face
unclouded by the ever-more estranged
chaff of ages sweeping through the place –
gold and gesso; coats and cameras;

and travel firms trying to bridge the space.
But as chaff too I'll follow my kind
as they wind the genius-hung labyrinth;
Giotto's goddess can never leave the mind
but neither can these I watch wander round
with an indifference magnificent, profound.

St Wilfrid's

After the service with Eric,
bible-studying in the annex
conscientiously, his voice parabling the ceiling,
nattering himself into radiance,
the misery of Sunday
dropped on us quietly,
hoarding our heads like a mantle.

One week, the vicar announced Eric's engagement
to Eileen, who led the girls.
We spun round as one. At the back,
segregated by the aisle, their smiles returned
our amazement.
We sung a stunned thanksgiving . . . .

I got out soon after, I think.
I couldn't take the vision,
that cosy hallowed complicity
of salvation and slippers,
hallelujah and Horlicks and
epilogue-sped increase after lights-out.

The Bodybuilder

I watch him contorting beside the pool,
examining each limb; arms kneaded
and suppled like new shoes, legs tried
for support, like planks across streams.
Even vanity has vanished by now:
he expands and contracts in oblivion.

Think of being him! Laden with body
like a banker's bag or landlord's wallet,
wary with plenty; carefully weighing up
all sport's or sex's muscular consequences;
the dinosaur walk, matter bounding
about him at every step, anchoring mind;
massively opposite weeds in the tube,
wedged in seat, secretly flexing forearms,
hypnotised by mirrors, full-length shop-fronts.

Strange the different courses between coming and going;
if an afterlife, strange preparations.
For what reward or penalty
could possibly cap this life?
His muscles' ghostly contours
allotted an Elysian knoll apart,
where the mad dance of fist to forehead
continues indefinitely? – (where bands
of strolling philosophers divide and re-group
around him, discoursing) . . . .

February 1982

Steve, I saw you today:
You were about sixty,
I'd say, sitting on a chair
In the library, unaware
Of a proposed tome across your knees;
Quietly offended you sprinkled round
That familiar edgy stare,
As if you found the air itself
Vulgar and conspiring,
And your being there
(As with all your surroundings)
A rather tasteless joke.

It must be five years since we met
But after college it wasn't the same –
That brief hiatus of wildness
For two polite suburban boys
Becoming polite suburban men:
You were summoned by a suit
And herded to a London office,
I trailed on with research;
When we met we couldn't see
How floor-rolling midnight fights
And hilarious verbal idiocies
Could team with our final roles.

You resented and I researched.
Now seeing you today as you'll be,
Near the end, showed how destiny
Holds no late harvest; I thought
Life was a gradual fruiting
Until wisdom waved its golden ears
Through benign, final summers.
Unemployed with two degrees
I realise now what firm roots
Diffidence has, what insistent flowers
Bind me to you and your elder twin:
To all those who are not like trees
But blossom as only love can approve.

Summer of '82

London literary do: wine on a patio
enclosed by white-walled Kensington,
a nebula of the not-quite-famous
adrift among furniture, back outside
me and briefly-coupled German girl
talk Fassbinder under dying twilight.
Or rather, Fassbinder's death. Or rather
I oil her talk by chipping in bits
fished up from the rather low stocks
the mind's junk-shop has on F. Until:
(in her almost faultless enunciation)
'He was burning the candle at both ends.'

That quaint phrase stripped down years.
The sixth-form again, Boff at the front
opening the portal to Keats's odes
with the same words. 'He knew he was dying
and had to get his life's work done.'
What rich anticipations were woven
in that world of blazers and ties!
– as of moments under London twilight;
but look on that picture then on this
for a pocket definition of catastrophe:
to have talked of Keats at eighteen –
to be talking Fassbinder at thirty.

'Glory be to God for dappled things . . . '

Lino too:

an ocean of strange scuffed lands;
mountain-smudges on a white chart,
shoals and coral-reef sands.
I can see Victorian explorers
tracing it with their hands:
their amazed inner conjectures
where nervous calligraphic coastlines
show continents petering away.

My childhood rekindles
on this public-building floor:
cosy evenings in a bedroom den,
encyclopaedia, star-map, bird-guide,
The Picture Book of World Knowledge,
adventure stories about lagoons
(adventure stories favoured lagoons).
That far country is hidden now
behind gradual high-rise blocks:
exam on exam, narrowing degrees,
concrete roads marked 'Career'
and no road going back.

Only sudden transits: for now this floor
is gaseous infinity where stiletto heels
have stamped slow suns in their thousands.

Washing

Strange that in our discreet suburb
where houses are bastions of privacy
gardens should burst into weekly bloom
with rows of most intimate garments.
Sexual histories strewn on the wind:
not-quite-washed-out stains and blood,
frilly incitements in scarlet and black,
tiny triangles embroidered with hearts
speak sensational night manoeuvres.
But the lacrimae rerum of laundry!
Here, the brave underpants of youth,
tight, yet elastic for times of expansion;
there, hoisted in shapeless surrender,
the vast flapping whites of old age.

Summer '84

My father-in-law adored a drought.
At the first sign of a sun in stasis,
cracked soil, rumours on the radio,
he'd mobilise an army of buckets
and scurry all over the house, planning
complex campaigns of tap and bowl.
He could charm water from room to room
through a hundred different uses:
faces, socks, windows, the car, the loo
all downstream from each other. When
that final basinful of brown scum
was scattered over the garden plants,
you could see water in his own eyes
aching to join it, or else the worry
there was yet another function
he might have made it flow through . . . .

Yes, in droughts I've studied his face –
his eyes lit up by sheets of fire
as news comes in that things get worse;
and the fantasy inside his head
of an enormous toasted England,
himself appointed to a mountain crest
to conduct the State's last trickles,
an orchestra of pipes and channels.

At night he awoke from nasty dreams
that the summer's first raindrop
hung over his head like a sword.

On Completing His Thirtieth Year

Auntie's non-index-linked birthday present
is due tomorrow – three faithful decades
of single pound notes slipped inside cards.
This complicated trail of London addresses
could never shake them off: white oblongs
cast over the tiles of ill-lit hallways
always include hers. Friends increase
and decline; the sad routine of her message
'Love Auntie', her card, her pound, stay.

Golden years of childhood tolled away
in golden digits, till 'You are 9':
a sketch of thrushes' eggs, a penny black,
model plane, microscope and pirate's hat
presumably confirmed it. For puberty
designs of radios and racing-bikes
dancing round the Eiffel Tower, until
artists' impressions of maturity arrived:
an Aston Martin and 12-bore shotgun,
with intimations of sleek spoiled women
adrift in the wake of bachelorhood
floating around the card's perimeters.

Aston Martins have come for five years now –
I'll pick one up tomorrow off the tiles
and open it en route to the bus-stop.
To be brightly told for three decades
that 'Someone as nice as you' deserves
'What they want the whole year through!'
narrows no gap between life and art.
If only exclamation marks were God
the gap might go – at seventy, say:
I open the door of Honeysuckle Cottage
bound on a fishing-trip; there's Auntie's card,
by now a shot of some serene evening,
a fellow in water up to his waders
plucking a salmon off a shining lake.
Me, in fact. Pocketing the pound,
I select car, bait, girl and tackle
then zoom off into the sunset.

Love Poem at Thirty

O when will I see Uncle James again
Sniffing the stars, or the fried-fish man
Fantasmally white as his own cod,
His golden light-bulb burning late
To an empty suburb? My Northern Lights,
Always crossing the horizon of my mind
Like mind's zodiac, what sun is this
That has risen and put you to flight?

Emigréd in London, I could be seen
Communing with you at any dusk
In solitary Finchley avenues; there I
Have seen Geoff Boycott batting in the sky,
Or rode the chute of the setting sun
Gloriously dissatisfied. Who'd have thought
My provincial Muse in clogs and shawl
Would fade so meekly, at love's call?

But my love shook her busy blond beams
Into all my corners, stripping me down
To the bare bright room of fulfilment.
At times I still wander to the window
And dabble with earth and sky, glimpsing
That vanished romance of elsewhere,
Its lost heroes. Now why did love shrink
All times and places into this square?

But time shrinks love too: a harder truth.
The groves of adolescence go down,
Their deities scarper into the shade
Of newer, yearning minds. My blessings on
That fleeing flat-capped pantheon;
And now I'll turn back to my light.
If I get used to seeing straight
I'll give these walls a new coat of paint.